T0375599

Who Is the
Victim In
Divorce?

Dr. Gilbert H. Edwards, Sr.

authorHOUSE®

AuthorHouse™
1663 Liberty Drive
Bloomington, IN 47403
www.authorhouse.com
Phone: 833-262-8899

Published by AuthorHouse   09/06/2024

ISBN: 979-8-8230-3211-7 (sc)
ISBN: 979-8-8230-3210-0 (e)

Dedicated to my wife, Dorothy Edwards
for 60 years of marriage.

PREFACE

I have focused on marriage and divorce and found that there are many people who get hurt because of it. Who is the victim? Marriage is the relationship between man and woman under whose shadow alone, there can be true reverence for the mystery, dignity and sacredness of life. Its sacredness goes back to the very birth of man.

In the first pre-Christian century, there was a fundamental cleavage in the religious schools of Palestine regarding divorce. The dispute turned over the interpretation of Deuteronomy 24:1; but as so often in theological controversy, the words of the sacred text were merely the pegs upon which to hand conflicting theories of life on the part of the recusants. The School of Shammai maintained that a marriage could be dissolved only by unchastity on the part of the wife, because adultery alone sapped the foundation of marriage and made its continuance impossible.

CONTENTS

INTRODUCTION

For many years, I have been counseling marriages and trying to solve marriage problems. God, in the appointment of marriage, united the husband and wife to have the same interests, and to share each other's comforts and sorrows. God hath yoked them together, so the Word is, and it is very significant. When marriage was instituted, sin and death had not entered; therefore, neither the sinful cause of separation, nor the natural dissolutions were referred to, and in all other respects, the union is to be considered as indissoluble. As what Moses had directed respecting a writing of divorcement, he showed them that this was not a command, but a permission; a mere judicial regulation, a departure from the meaning of the Moral Law, on account of the hardness of their hearts. I stated that because I am in total agreement of it. What God joint together, let no man (human) come between.

CHAPTER I

THE TEACHING OF JESUS CHRIST CONCERNING DIVORCE

Jesus answering the question, "Is it lawful for a man to put away (divorce) his wife for every cause?" For every cause; whenever he chooses. In Mark 10, verse 4 He states, "Have ye not read; Genesis 1:27.

Verse 6: One flesh; they are so united as to be no longer two, but one, each being a part of the other. Ephesians 5:28: He that loveth his wife, loveth himself. They ought to be one in views, affections, and interests; and for a man to break such a union as this by putting away (divorce) his wife for every cause, is wrong,

Verse 7: A writing of divorcement. Deuteronomy 24:1: unseemly thing in her; women is a moral personality and not a thing, that a man may hand over to another, and then take back again at pleasure.

Verse 8: "because of the hardness of your hearts, suffered you to put away (divorce) your wives; suffered; he did not direct it, or suffer it in any such sense as to imply that God approved of it or that it was right. It was a civil regulation of a civil government suffered for a time on account of the wickedness of men, and in order to prevent the greater evils which that wickedness would otherwise have occasioned. It was a regulation as to the mode of putting away (divorce) or not to justify that wrong practice, but to lessen, in some measure, its evils. Not so from the beginning, and in all its stages, this putting away (divorce) "for every cause" of one's wife was a violation of the will of God, as manifested in his works and his Word.

Verse 9; I say unto you; whosoever shall put away (divorce) his wife, except it be for fornication, and shall marry another, committed adultery. Jesus' teaching and the early apostolic church allowed no scope whatsoever for divorce.

To summarize this teaching of Jesus; Jesus' view is that marriage is indissoluble and there is no legal ground for divorce; in view of the fact that marriage had been brought about by God himself, it could not be dissolved by any secular authority. In the beginning divorce was not permitted. Jesus was referring here to the initial phase of man's history or at least to the time before the Mosaic Law. In any case, the essential meaning of this phrase is that God did not have this as his original intention when he established the institution of marriage by his creation of mankind, as man and woman.

Woman is to be the helpmate of man. A wife is man's other self, all that man's nature demands for its completion physically, socially and spiritually. In married life, man finds his trust and most lasting happiness; and only through married life does human personality reach its highest fulfillment. A man shall leave his father and mother and cleave to his wife (Genesis 2:24). Note, that is man who is to cleave to his wife and not the woman, physically the weaker, who is to cleave to her husband; because in the higher sphere of the soul, woman is the ethical and spiritual superior of man. He who has not a wife, abides without good, help, joy and blessings. He who has no wife cannot be considered a whole man. Just as one step shatters the glass, so can one act of unfaithfulness forever destroy the holiness and happiness of the home.

I hate divorce, is the divine message by the Prophet Malachi (2:16). The very altar weeps for one who divorces the wife of his youth. In the New Testament, divorce was to be permitted, for the one and sole reason of adultery. God hates those who divorce their wives (Malachi 2:16). If you hate her, curb your desirous spirit. Even though it is preferable to divorce an unloved wife than to remain married to her and continue hating her, the best alternative is to curb your desirous spirit. Jesus said that the only reason God allowed Moses to make any provision for divorce was a concession to human sin. God's intention is that marriage is for a life-time, as seen in Genesis 1:2. Jesus affirmed God's intention for permanent marriage. He denied the husband's assumed right to divorce a woman for any reason. He warned husbands not to ruin a wife's reputation by divorcing her. He charged husbands with adultery, when they divorced an innocent wife and remarried. He placed guilt on a woman whose sexual sins destroyed a marriage.

He limited or even prohibited divorce, as part of God's will for marriage. Divorce involves missing the will of God for the marriage partner.

God intended marriage to meet the basic human need of love and companionship. The expression describing the companionship literally means "a helper corresponding to him", or "a helper alongside of him"; a beautiful relationship which God intended between husband and wife. That is why the man is to be sure he finds the right mate. One of God's basic purposes for marriage is companionship. Companionship is a feeling of fellowship or friendship. The basic implication of the text focuses on the similarity of man and woman, and on their mutual need for each other. (Genesis 2:18-24) Because of their similarity, the man and the woman can marry and establish a one-flesh union that takes priority over all other relations. True human love involves and is based upon life commitment. It can also lead the husband and wife to work hard to establish a life-long relationship. True love leads to self-sacrifice. The relationship which should exist between husband and wife is one of complete giving of each other (Song of Solomon 2:16).

When the husband and wife sins together, the marriage suffers (Jeremiah 44:19). When values are wrong and activities are sinful, the individual and the marriage suffers a long and close love for each other. When there is loss of a marriage partner, it may be the world's loneliest and saddest feeling; humans cannot provide sufficient comfort. I know that what I am about to say is not truly understandable, but infidelity does not always destroy the love of a faithful spouse. True love leaves one to struggle to regain the love of the unfaithful one, paying whatever price that may be necessary (Hosea 3:1-3).

What is marriage? Marriage is that relationship between man and woman under whose shadow alone, there can be true reverence for the mystery, dignity and sacredness of life. Marriage is the conjunction of two loves in one mind. It shall first be explained what the nature of this conjunction is: the mind consists of two parts of which one is called "the understanding", and the other "the will." When these two parts act as one, they are called one mind. The husband acts the part which is called "the understanding", (which is live with your wife according to knowledge – I Peter 3:7) and the wife acts the part which is "the will". This conjunction, which is of the interiors, descends into the lower things that are of their body, it is perceived and felt as love. This love derives its origin from the conjunction of two in one mind. This is called cohabitation; however, it is said that they are not two, but one. For this reason, a marriage pair is not called two, but one. There is such a conjunction of the husband and wife even in the inmost, who are of their minds, coming from creation itself. They who are in love, that is true conjugal, look to what is eternal because there is eternity in that love. It being eternal is from the fact that love increases with the wife and wisdom with the husband to eternal. The husband must have wisdom and understanding of how to deal with his wife (I Peter 3:7). The prayer of the husband must not be hindered by misunderstanding in the relationship.

The purpose of marriage is two-fold: posterity and companionship. Posterity - the duty of building a home and rearing a family (Genesis 1:28), "Be fruitful and multiply." Companionship - is the other primary end of the marriage institution. The woman is to be the helpmate of the man. A wife is a man's other self and all that man's nature demands for its completion physically, socially and spiritually. In marriage alone, can man's need for physical and social companionship be directed to holy ends! In marriage life, man finds his trust and most lasting happiness; and only through marriage life does the human personality reach its highest fulfillment. A man shall leave his mother and father and cleave to his wife. A man who has no wife, abides without goodness, help, joy and blessings, or atonement. Marriage is part of God's purpose in creation and should not be forbidden. God ordained marriage and procreation, at Creation. Everything He created was very good (Genesis 1:26).

Marriage is ordered to the good of the spouses and to the procreation and education of children. The love of the husband and wife, and the begetting of children create among members of the same family, personal relationships and primordial responsibilities. A man and a woman united in marriage, together with their children, form a family. Try to build up your marriage and home life in every possible way. Build each other up in personality and in happiness. Marriage calls for two kinds of love in order to bring fulfillment. It requires somewhat of the romantic love that drew you two together. Each must continue to feel that the other is special and precious. Each marriage is a personal relationship, and it is what the two persons make it.

CHAPTER II

DIVORCE IS A PAINFUL WORD

It smarts deeply in each one who cherishes the sanity of marriage. It is a word that cannot be ignored. It will not go away. Jesus' speech is straightforward. And His teaching on the subject remains our standard to this very hour,

> Jesus states; "Haven't you read". He replied, "that at the beginning the Creator made them male and female, and said, for this reason a man will leave his father and mother and be united to his wife, and the two will become one flesh. So, they are no longer two, but one. Therefore, what God has joined together, let man not separate." (Matthew 19:4-6)

The matter of divorce was a great contention among the Jews. For some, the thought of dissolving a marriage, except for the cause of adultery, was not even to be contemplated.

But for others, the possibility of a legal divorce hinged on the smallest offense of a wife-including such things as yelling, house-keeping, spoiling a meal, speaking disrespectfully and losing eye appeal.

How Jesus answered the most humanity question: "Does God permit a man to divorce his wife for any reason at all?" Jesus quoted God's clear position. Marriage was (and is) to be the most intimate union found on earth. Jesus quoted Genesis 2:23,24). The husband and wife are joined together in marriage to form a unique and single expression of life, with each person complementing and fulfilling the other person. And no one is granted permission to sever this lifelong attachment. Based upon the scripture text and words of Jesus, the following points are:

(1) The only justified basis for a divorce, in Jesus' teaching, was adultery. Repentance, forgiveness and renewed love can rectify any otherwise hopeless marriage. The innocent party may choose to divorce the mate, and in such cases is free to remarry.

(2) If a person divorce someone without proper justification, then any remarriage constitutes adultery.

(3) While the weight of the discussion on divorce often falls on guilty women, Jesus also taught that the same principles for divorce apply to guilty men, as well.

When a man puts a wife out, it makes her cry and it makes her feel unworthy. When there is a divorce, the family separates and when that happens, sometimes the husband would lead the son against his own mother. The son begins to treat and talk disrespectfully to his mother, the same as he does. After she had put out all the love, the best she could, and now it was for nothing. Some people want you to love or treat them the way they love or treat you, but you can only give what you have. Divorce causes many tears.

When Joseph thought that Mary had cheated on him by committing adultery, he wanted to put her away privily. The Bible states, ". . . when as his mother Mary was espoused to Joseph, before they came together, she was found with child of the Holy Ghost. Then Joseph, her husband, being a just man and not willing to make her a public example, was minded to <u>put her away privily</u>. (Matthew 1:18-19)

Mary was espoused to Joseph; engaged to be married to him, before they were actually married (by the ceremonial act). They were married but had to come together for the ceremonial law to complete the marriage. The marriage, a public example; not willing to have her punished according to the Law (Deuteronomy 22:21). Put her away (divorce) privily, by writing a bill of divorcement, according to Deuteronomy 24:1.

Joseph did not want to disgrace Mary by putting her through an open shame. Joseph did not want to expose or defame his wife, Mary. Betrothal vows were binding as marriage even though the couple did not live together until the wedding

Dr. Gilbert H. Edwards, Sr.

(Deuteronomy 22:24), where the betrothal virgin is called a "wife." In accordance with Jewish legislation, which provided for divorce rather than stoning the woman, Joseph planned to divorce Mary because of her apparent sexual unfaithfulness. Divorce is painful for the victim of divorce.

CHAPTER III

MOSES' TEACHING CONCERNING MARRIAGE AND DIVORCE

He who falsely accuses his wife of unchastity during betrothal shall be rebuked, fined, and he loses the right even to divorce her. Betrothal in Bible times united the bridal couple as husband and wife for all purposes, save living together; and any infidelity on the part of the wife was considered adultery (Deuteronomy 22:13, 14, 23). In considering these plain-spoken laws (verses 13-21), it is just to remember that they represent an upward stage in the struggle against the animal passions of men.

In principle proven adultery between a man and another married or betrothed woman was punished in Israel, both the guilty parties normally being put to death after trial (Deuteronomy 22:2-5). The wife was subject to her husband's rule, with the result that the third party had no right to her (Deuteronomy 20:5-7; 28:30). Marriage was a divine institution in which God Himself gave the woman to the man as his life's companion and placed her under his authority. No other man was therefore permitted to lay any claim to a married woman.

Initially, divorce was the almost unrestricted right of the man. The woman, on the other hand, was neither able nor permitted to repudiate her husband (Judges 19:2-10). The Law, in the spirit of the Mosaic Cult of Yahweh, moderated this unrestricted right and regulated it. A man might repudiate his wife only when some indecency was found in her (Deuteronomy 24:1). In that case, it was sufficient for the husband to give her a bill of divorce, in which he declared that she was henceforth no longer his wife (Deuteronomy 24:1-4; Jeremiah 3:8). With this, the marriage was annulled, and both were free to marry.

From its conception, Judaism has always recognized two purposes in marriage; both spelled out in the opening passage of the scripture, "The first is the fulfillment of the first commandment: be fruitful and multiply (Genesis 1:28). The second function of marriage is that of companionship. The Laws governing family life play a prominent role in Jewish survival. A woman who was divorced because she committed adultery is forbidden to marry the man with whom the adulterous act was committed. A man is forbidden to remarry a woman whom he has divorced, is she has subsequently been married to another man, who then died for divorced her (Deuteronomy 24:1-5). Moses' Law is that if a man marries a woman, and if she displeases him, or if he has evidence of sexual misconduct on her part, he shall write her a bill of divorce, place it in her hand releasing her from his household. When she leaves his household, she may go and marry another man.

If a couple is dating and cannot control their sexual desires, then they should marry. The woman's need is an important criterion. All priorities must be taken into account, as a couple considers marriage. The needs of both partners deserve equal consideration,

Moses

All prohibited marriages are voided such as:

(1) A man may not marry his mother, grandmother, and descendants. The mother of his grandfather; his stepmother, the wife of his paternal grandfather and of his descendants; and the wife of his maternal grandfather.

(2) His daughter, granddaughter, great-granddaughter and her descendants; his daughter-in-law, the wife of his son's son and descendants, and the wife of his daughter's son.

(3) His wife' mother or grandmother, the mother of his father-in-law and descendants.

(4) His wife's daughter or granddaughter, and descendants.

(5) His sister, half-sister, his full or half-brother's wife (divorced or widowed); and the full or half-sister of his divorced wife in her lifetime.

(6) His aunt or uncle's wife (divorced or widowed); whether the uncle be the full, or half-brother of his father or mother.

(7) A married woman, unless permission has been given; and his divorce wife after her remarriage (her second husband) having died or divorced her.

(8) Anyone who is not a member of the Jewish faith; the issue of an incestuous union; the married woman guilty of adultery with him; and the woman whose husband died childless, until chalitzah has been performed. A Kohen may not marry a divorced woman, a chalitzah widow, or a proselyte. The marriage ceremony states:

> "I require and charge you both, as ye will answer at the dreadful Day of Judgement when the secrets of all hearts shall be disclosed, that if either of you know of any impediment as to why ye may not be lawfully joined together in matrimony, ye do now confess it. For be ye well assured, that if any persons are joined together otherwise than as God's word doth allow, their marriage is not lawful (voided)."

A man may marry:

(1) His stepsister, his stepfather's wife (divorced or widowed), his niece; and his full or half-brother's or sister's daughter-in-law.

(2) His cousin; his stepson's wife (divorced or widowed); and his deceased wife's sister.

A woman may not marry:

(1) Her father, grandfather and descendants; her stepfather; and the husband of her grandmother, and of her descendants.

(2) Her son, grandson, great-grandson; her son-in-law, and the husband of her granddaughter and descendants.

(3) Her husband's father, or grandfather; and the father of her father-in-law; and descendants; and the father of her mother-in-law.

(4) Her husband's son or grandson, and descendants.

(5) Her brother; half-brother; her full or half sister's divorced husband in her sister's lifetime; and her husband's brother and her nephew.

(6) A married man, unless permission has been given; and her divorced husband after the death or divorce of her second husband.

(7) Anyone who is not a member of the Jewish faith; the incestuous union (Mamzer); and the man guilty of adultery with her as a married woman.

A woman may marry:

(1) Her cousin; and her deceased sister's husband, whether full or half-sister.

(2) Her stepbrother, and her stepmother's former husband.

(3) Her uncle

CHAPTER IV

WHAT PROMPS A PERSON TO MARRY

"If any man takes a wife, and
go in unto her and hate her"
(Deuteronomy 22:13)

And hate her; the man entered in marriage merely for
the satisfaction of his passions and then turned against
her by a revulsion of feeling frequent in such characters
(Deuteronomy 21:14; II Samuel 13:15). Some men marry
to have his wife as a female war-captive – to use her as
a slave. Don't get rid of her after you have humbled her.
After trying to get rid of her, it brings shame to her and to
the public she seems to be unattractive. Some men refuse
to work, will marry for money, or they want a woman
who will take care of them. They marry because they have
nowhere to go. Some women marry because they want
someone to father their children. Some people are married
because their parents forced them to marry. Some marry
because the woman got pregnant. Some marry to take

revenge, because the one they loved married someone else. Some marry just for companionship; they are growing old and lonely. Some women get married because they are having babies out of wed lock.

Paul states in I Corinthians, chapter seven; "to avoid fornication, let every man have his own wife", that is to get married. Some people marry because they cannot control their sexual passions. Satan tempts people to sexual sin by using the lack of self-control to lead them to immorality. Many people marry without love for one another. There is a time when one person loves, but the other doesn't. I believe it is because they have not married the right person. So, they marry for other reasons, and not because of love.

Sometimes, God tells a person who to marry. Hosea's marriage became a prophetic sign symbolizing Judah's rejection of God in favor of Baal. God commanded Hosea to take a prostitute for a wife (Hosea 1:2). Go, marry a prostitute who has children from her prostitution. A heavy domestic sorrow darkened Hosea's life. He had married a woman called Gomer; and she rendered him deeply unhappy. He found that he had wasted his love on a profligate woman. She fled from his house and sunk lower and lower until she became the slave – concubine of another. But Hosea's love was proof even against faithlessness and dishonor. He, the deeply grieved husband, buys her back from slavery and brings her back into his house. Hosea's feelings toward Gomer is what led him to an over whelming spiritual discovery; if he could love a faithless wife so tenderly and patiently, what must the love of God be toward His people? And if he did not despise that love and patience, it would awaken Gomer's better nature.

CHAPTER V

THE WIFE AS THE VICTIM OF DIVORCE

Marriage is not a trade-in business. This passage (Malachi 2:13-16) is the strongest statement in the Old Testament against divorce among the covenant people. Malachi condemned the practice of divorcing older wives married within the covenant community to marry younger women, or women of the mixed tribes, who had remained in Israel during the Babylonian captivity. The prophet anticipated the teaching of Jesus that all divorce is contrary to God's original intention for marriage (Matthew 19:4-9). The woman who marries a man that does not love her, will not be treated as a wife, which will bring about an unfriendly home, as two strangers in the same house.

> "When a man taketh a wife, and marries her, then it cometh to pass, if she finds no favor in his eyes, because he hath found some unseemly thing in her, that he writeth her a bill of divorcement and giveth her

hand, and sendeth her out of the house …"
(Deuteronomy 24)

"Over him who divorces the wife of his
youth, even the altar of God sheds tears."

Some people may not consider divorce a sin; it recognizes
it as a tragedy. Each divorce is a tombstone of high hopes
once held by two young people. Hopes that have dissolved
in bitterness and hostility. The unhappiness of the adult
partner is only one part of this massive burden of misery.
There are thousands of innocent victims of discord, the
children of divorce, who lack the security and guidance
of two parents and a stable home. Marriage is not a
trade-in business, changing from one woman to another.
Some husbands try to make merchandise of their wives by
divorcing her because he sees another woman that he desires
(Exodus 21:8). He deals with her as a slave. The Bible says
that he must not reduce her in the home ot the level of a
bondswoman. Otherwise, don't shame her or dishonor her.
Jesus warned husbands not to ruin a wife's reputation by
divorcing her. He charged husbands with adultery, when
they divorce an innocent wife and remarry. Jesus placed
guilt on a woman whose sexual sins destroyed a marriage.
Women always seems to be the victim of divorce.

John states in chapter eight – Jesus was teaching in the
Temple Court, and people were coming to Him in a
constant procession to hear His words and to ask Him
questions. The session was interrupted by a dignifying, but
overbearing group of man who pushed their way through
the circle, leading with them a woman, placing her squarely

in the middle of the crowd. This group of men said to Jesus," Teacher, this woman hath been taken in adultery, in the very act." Now, the Law of Moses commands us to stone such. Where was the man? If she was really caught in the very act, why did they not bring the man involved that he might share the guilt and condemnation? No one should commit adultery. In the sight of God, it is wrong and Moses' Law states that both the man and woman shall be put to death.

Marriage is not merely a contract. It is consecration, and adultery is far more than merely an offence against one of the parties to a contract. It is an offense against the divine command proclaimed at Sinai; and constitutes the annihilation of holiness in marriage.

CHAPTER VI

DIVORCE EFFECTS THE CHILDREN

The first and most important classroom in the school of life is the home. Both father and mother are expected to assume the responsibility for training and nurturing the minds of the children (Proverbs 1:8). Parental teachings are basic to family living and to society's large educational program. Such teachings should lead to commitment to the Lord. When or if a father walks out on his children, then there is no parental training as to what God commanded. What does it feel like to be raised in a single-family home? The meaning is to be raised by just one parent. The love between a father and son is damaged because of divorce. The father not only walks out on his wife, but also his son's life. Who does the son hate, his mother or his father, for the divorce? It may be that after the father leaves, then a stranger will enter his life. Is it the same if a stranger takes you to a ball game, rather than your own father? Who knows what it feels like to lose a father and son love? It must be a hurtful feeling, after raising and being with your son for many years and then, something comes in between. After many years, Sarah said to her husband, "Abraham, get rid of that bond woman and her son, which is Abraham's son." (Genesis 21:10) Early the next morning, Abraham took some food and water and gave it to Hagar, and then sent her away with the boy, Abraham's son. That affected the child. The Bible says, God heard the boy crying. (Genesis 21:17) Divorce hurts!

Parental discipline helps young adults avoid tragic mistakes. When parents don't discipline their children, their lives will end up in tragic circumstances such as: jail, prison, stealing, drugs, strong drink, pregnancy or even murder. This means that the parents have failed and ruined the child's life. So, if the father divorces his wife and walks out from the home, then who is going to help discipline that child? Listen to this, if a man divorces his wife and marry another woman, then he will have two living wives. How will the child adapt to that? The child then will have two mothers. Which one will he love the most? Who would the child blame for the divorce, the father or the mother? Parenthood means devoting prime time to loving and taking children. How can that happen, if the father divorces his wife, and the wife moves into another State. What would that father and son relationship be like? The father will be neglecting the son of his rights as being disciplined by his father. If the wife remarries, then the child will have two fathers. Which one will he obey? Be sure that family life is not usurped so drastically by other concerns, mothers and fathers are faced with making the best choices for the use of their time when children are young. Before making a choice to divorce, the father and mother must first consider the welfare of their children.

Chapter VII

Paul's View Concerning Marriage And Divorce

Apostle Paul states, "And unto the married I command, yet not, I but the Lord; let not the wife depart from her husband: But and if she departs, let her remain unmarried, or be reconciled to her husband; and let not the husband put away his wife." (I Corinthians 7:10-11). "Not I, but the Lord; not Paul only, but Jesus Christ." (Matthew 5:32; 19:3-10) So, I Corinthians states, "Marriage is designed for permanence." Divorce must not be seen as an easy option to escape problems. Christians who are married to one another, should commit themselves to each other and to working out problems in the relationship. To do otherwise, goes against God's word.

Apostle Paul also states, "For the woman which hath a husband is bound by the law to her husband so long as he lives; but if the husband be dead, she is loosed from the law of her husband. So then if, while her husband liveth, she be married to another man, she should be called an adulteress;

but if her husband be dead, she is free from that law; so, she is no adulteress, though she be married to another man." (Romans 7:2-3)

Again, Apostle Paul states, ". . . it is good for a man not to touch (marry) a woman, nevertheless, to avoid *fornication*, let every man have his own wife, and let every woman have her own husband." (I Corinthians 7:1-2)

> His own wife – her own husband; no man is allowed by God to have at once more than one wife, and no woman to have more than one husband.

Paul explains problems in the marriage, such as "due benevolence." These words express the mutual duty of the husband and wife toward each other. Not power of her own body; not to live apart, even for a time, without mutual consent. Defraud ye not one the other; deprive not one another by separation, of any safeguard against temptation. Do nothing which shall tend to impurity or give Satan advantage over you.

The union of life for one man and woman in marriage is an appointment of God, designed for the continuance and benefit of humanity. All who are in proper circumstances and are so disposed ought to be permitted to form such a union; and all who do form it, should faithfully discharge their duties. Whatever increases temptation to evils, which marriage was designed to prevent, or renders it ineffectual for the purposes for which it was instituted, should be carefully avoided. The obligations, rights and privileges of marriage continue throughout life, notwithstanding any changes in religious character, which may take place in either of the parties; and married persons, wherever it be practicable consistently with duty, should live together, for the purpose of promoting each other's highest temporal and eternal good.

Men should continue, in the situation, in which God has placed them, and in the business, if it be moral and right, to which they are accustomed, unless without committing sin they can change them for the better. If they can, they are bound to do it, and in a manner accordant with the revealed will of God. No worldly circumstances should so disturb or occupy our minds, so to unfit us in any measure for duty; nor should we desire any more world enjoyment than God shall graciously give s in doing His will. So important is the institution of marriage, so honorable in all, and so numerous its blessings to those who faithfully discharge its duties; that those who, in the fear and love of God marry, though in troublous times, if their wishes had been different, it would have been better, at least for them, had they for a time remained married.

Chapter VIII

How To Keep Marriage Together

Husbands and wives are different. Pre-marital counseling helps to bring the differences together. Spouses cannot change each other personally, but they can learn to live with each other's differences. The creation of the two sexes is a part of the beneficial purpose of God. Marriage is mainly a physical relationship, but a union to which a man and a woman brings all they have and all they are. Physically they give themselves as they are made, and this physical giving is part of the total self-giving of marriage. The man and the woman are in so many ways alike that one sex can be made up with cosmetics to pass for the other. At the same time, they are so different that every cell in the body of each shows this difference and they have different roles to play. They need to understand these differences and to accept them as part of the excellence of life together. Those differences enter their daily relationships enabling them to stimulate, supplement, reinforce, help, and enjoy each other in countless ways. This mutual attractiveness of the sexes is constantly turning listlessness into vital interest, and sprinkling bits of poetry into the phase of everyday experience.

It would be hard to estimate how much of the finest in man is due to woman, and how much of the best in woman is due to man. The physical union symbolizes the fact that marriage is meant to be a splendid unity in difference. This union is not a mere biological necessity for the continuance of the race, nor a duty which one owes to each other. It is a symbol and expression of a unity of this man and woman in the entire range of their existence. The wife wants to be cuddled and loved rather than forced either physically or mentally. Her nature is such that love means everything to her and the tenderest and most intimate and physical expression of union may be made such as to thrill her whole being. On the other hand, let the wife not insult the husband who is keeping himself for her, by regarding his passion as something unworthy. This is an offence to his manhood and unworthy of her as a mature woman. For the husband, the art of sexual love making is to find the times when both can enter with splendid abandon into a passionate expression of their unity, and also to discourse the ways which are favorable to complete mutuality of this experience.

In both sexes, nature has provided a general pattern of success in marital union and a variety of possible variants of the pattern and its is highly desirable for both to secure complete expressions of sex as provided for in the nervous and glandular system. Chronic sexual dissatisfaction is detrimental to the wife's nervous health. The unself-fish husband thinks of this form of intimacy in its effect upon his wife as much as for his own sake, while the selfish man uses sex as a mere personal gratification and only aggravates his mate. He stimulates her sex passion, but leaves it unsatisfied, giving her a sense of being abused and exploited, rather than loved and treasured. So also, the wife may on an occasion fail to have sufficient consideration for her mate. If you find out that you married the wrong mate, learn to live with them and love them.

When a man marries, he should have a reasonable understanding of God's creature (woman). Similarly, when a woman marries, she should have a reasonable understanding of God's creature (man). Each should understand the sexual nature and needs of the other, and they should grow in this understanding during their years of marriage. In many cases, sexual maladjustment is not primarily a matter of sex, but a result of the fact that the man and woman do not sufficiently love, trust, and admire each other. Therefore, they cannot give themselves fully to each other. The root of their trouble is psychological or spiritual. The sexual relationship in marriage is so important that it calls for understanding. Be sure that when you marry, marry for love.

Unity of the whole man and woman, including their social, intellectual, esthetic, and spiritual values, and their life as creators of a home, and parents and shapers of young lives, is the more adequate goal of marriage with many whose marriages are. Equally valuable sexual unity must be won with patience, mutual understanding, and a deeper appreciation of each other. This may take time and may involve a gradual achievement of a bodily unity that symbolizes a unity of heart and mind toward which the two people strive with equal ardor. It is better even in the interest of sexual harmony for a husband and wife to have great mutual respect, consideration for each other, and a desire to give rather than to grasp happiness. Two people with such attitudes are sure to have a more meaningful sexual life, because they have something to express in contrast with a couple who merely know all the answers. If complete sexual fulfillment is not found in the early weeks or months of marriage, this is nothing to worry about. But if faulty adjustment persists for a long period, it is time then for the couple to consult a physician or another counselor well trained in understanding marital problems. It is certain that any individual or couple will make mistakes. It is not required that a marriage be free from mistakes, but that a woman and man have a loving spirit with a forgiving attitude where necessary.

Love is indispensable but love alone is not enough. Love must be guided by understanding and kept on the right path by steadfast loyalty to each other and to marriage. During courtship, a man and a woman should have made a good start toward the understanding of the two different personalities. Marriage should step-up the ability of each to identify himself with the thoughts, feelings, fears, hopes, joys, and sorrows of the other. As the days and years pass, a marriage can be improved, strengthened, and made more creative almost without limits. Many and varied combinations of personalities can succeed in marriage, if there is an understanding of their differences, acceptance of their differences and generous mutual appreciation of each other. For a man and woman to work their way into each other's modes of thinking and feeling is a part of their adjustment as husband and wife. It is for them to bring together the best that they have learned, family experiences and from they have gained in their years before marriage, and weave that best skillfully into the pattern of their new family.

When a husband and a wife come into the presence of God together, the things which trouble them shrink in the presence of infinite wisdom and love. Marriage is based on high appreciation. Love sees the other person at his best. The appraisal of love is like the estimate of Jesus Christ. He saw people at their best. He found more good in them than they found themselves. There was courage, loyalty, resourcefulness, and greatness in common people whom He attracted to Himself. Because He loved them and saw the best in them, the things which He saw in them became actual. Love and appreciation are forces. They help to bring into being the good in people. The wise husband, if he sees his wife's faults, sees them through glasses of tolerant love which at the same time makes her virtues seem bright and shining. Apostle Paul states, "Whatever is true, whatever is just, whatever is pure, whatever is lovely, whatever is gracious, if there be any excellence and if there is anything worthy of praise, think about these things." (Philippians 4:8) Love sees whatever is true, honorable, just, pure, lovely, gracious and worthy of praise and things about these things with gratitude and joy.

The love of a young husband and wife is a resource for building the family. It is substantial capital in which they can begin their marriage and it is further enriched by all the love they put into the daily experience of their home and their marriage. But there are also liabilities. Thoughtless acts, harsh words, misunderstandings, and offences reduce the validity of the marriage. The ones who hurt each other more and more drift apart and finally swell the unhappy ranks in the divorce courts. Many other couples, however, with no fewer adjustment to make hold back their criticisms or temper them with kindness. They always try to put more sweet than bitter into the dish of their marriage. One who dishes out much appreciation and only a modest amount of criticism, and that at propitious moments is likely to be a pleasant person to live with. Two such who are at least moderately well suited for each other will build a fellowship worth keeping through life. They will be bound together by inner ties stronger than marriage laws and will live in an atmosphere pleasant with happy association. They will hold together, not because any law says they must, but because each has become a part of the other and either feels incomplete without the other. As years passed, they looked back. It was for better or for worse; richer or poorer; or in sickness and in health; till death us do part.

Marriage is a relationship of mutual superiority. Each individual is superior to each other at some point. The uniqueness and individuality of each is a precious thing. The technique of a good marriage is not to discount each other because of differences, but to treasure each other even more just because we are different. Every man is united with one who is wiser than he is in some issues; and he is wiser than she is at some point. Using their superiorities to supplement and enrich each other, they can be a wonderful team. But using their different kinds of strength to pull against each other or to see who is boss, they tie the same with no score on either side. Rather they check and frustrate each other and the stronger they are the more miserable they may make each other. When two people work together, there is still another gain in this glad acceptance of mutual superiority. Each is finding what it means to love; not only with romantic emotions of youth, but also with the mature joy of two who make life richer for each other and each becomes a finer person. Now the wife can say, "He found the best in me." It is a bad thing to marry the wrong mate and live in the same house for years and not love each other, not talking love but only business.

Here are some things to strive for to make a better marriage:

(1) Remember that as married people, we are still lovers and should be resourceful in expressing our love.

(2) Remember to stand by and for each other, we do not attack each other, we sustain each other. "A home divided against itself cannot stand."

(3) Let us express our love, undaring and mutual respect in our tones, words, and acts.

(4) Do things together that both can enjoy so that our lives will be bound together by shared interests and pleasant memories of good times together.

(5) Cultivate the habit of thinking of events and circumstances, not as they affect oneself, but as they affect the other.

(6) Apologize as soon as possible after one has said or done something which has hurt the other.

(7) Be rooters for each other in those matters that mean much to one and little to the other.

(8) Think of love as a gift of God and at the same time, as an achievement in your lives together. Love is the true wealth of our home.

(9) Bring God into the experience of every day so that your home life may be enriched with the love and truth of God.

(10) Deal with the children in an atmosphere of affection and unity.

(11) When differences arise, find how to use these in such a way that the family will be enriched by the different points of view and at the same time will pull together.

(12) Don't put each other on the defensive. We married not to fight our way through life, but to live our way into the finest experiences. Try to build up your marriage and home life in happiness and build up the personalities of your children by giving them a

> good example and an atmosphere of love and trust in your home.

Marriage calls for two kinds of love to bring fulfillment rather than disappointment. It still requires something of the romantic love that drew the two together. Each must continue to feel that the other is special and precious. They should keep up the spirit of courtship all their lives, neither taking the other for granted and not assuming that the love of the other is one's due. Neither should they expect love to take care of itself without any attention, and so to provide some magical and automatic success for their marriage. Each marriage is a personal relationship, and it is what the two people make it. Marriage is not merely feeling joy in each other, but also and especially giving joy to each other. Marriage is partly made up of poetic elements and partly of prose passages unless, however people learn how to get the meaning of the prose, they are not likely to have the poetry very long.

Marriage love is love woven into a pattern of living. It has in it the elements of understanding and of truly passionate kindness. It is rich in the many-sided joys because each is more concerned with giving joy, than with grasping it for himself. And joys are most truly experienced when they are most fully shared. It is a Law of Life that we receive most when we also give. The complete love toward which the marriage man and woman must grow and strive is much more substantial, dependable, and pleasing than the mere romantic excitement, which some may find so ephemeral because they depend upon that alone. Married love takes account of all the varied needs of the two who make it up. Such a marriage is not less rewarding emotionally because it is grown up. Married love is concerned with a nourishing diet which fulfills the needs of our whole nature, physically, mentally, socially, esthetically, and spiritually. Let the married person, therefore, keep the favor of love in his daily work, in the service which he performs, in the social experiences which means more because they are shared, and in that emotional security, which is based on firm and loyal ties.

The decisions which keep marriage going must be made within and not merely as it were, for us, by some automatic functioning of our emotions. Marriage love is love put into circulation in daily life. A woman does not need to have every man think she is beautiful, if her husband recognizes her real beauty. It is more desirable to be beautiful at home and less noticed in public, than to be beautiful to the world in general and unlovely at home. It is a finer achievement for a man to win and hold the steadfast love of one woman than to turn the head of many. How a husband and wife look at each other is more important than how they look to each other. How they look to each other can never be a matter of unconcern, but ultimately how they look at each other determines how they look to each other. Two persons who have looked at each other with kindness and appreciation through the years and have lived together beautifully will be beautiful to each other even when she has lost the "school-girl" complexion and his "hair" is not as it once was.

Tensions in marriage are an outcome of being intense, and marriage is an intense affair. However, there is a way of living together, which permits us still to remain intense and yet relaxed toward each other. We can become so well harmonized that we pull together and not against each other. Home is the school of excellence learning how to get along together. Human nature itself helps because those faults that make it hard for people to cooperate are more than matched by impulses of love and cooperativeness which prompt men and women to adjust their differences and share their lives together. But personal artistry and loving purpose must carry on where human nature provides merely a beginning.

The purpose of two people in their marriage life is a joint purpose rather than a competition of independent purpose. In their major aims, they are one. Differences represent divergent conceptions as to how their aims are to be carried out. Since their aims have the quality of mutuality, a part of the value of everything they do is that they do it happily together. It has become almost unthinkable to either of them to have purpose which he must push through at the risk of hurting the other and marrying the harmony of their life together. These two people have gained a type of maturity that has not yet been clearly defined. It might yet be called "affectional maturity". It goes beyond mere emotional maturity, important as it is, just like love itself is more than emotions. Love involves one's values and life purposes. Affectional maturity characterizes people who have made the maintaining of creative affectionate fellowship an end, in itself, and who direct events and circumstances as a means toward that end. Their life may not always be unruffled, yet this attitude gives a stability that makes people steadfast in their love and always warm on their kindness. When people are affectionately mature, the primary purpose of each is to bring happiness to the other.

Things That Help Marriages

1. Gaining a mature conception of love.
2. Planning for children and cooperating in caring for them.
3. Using one's differences to supplement and stimulate each other.
4. Keeping a sense of humor and cheerfulness.
5. Keeping up the spirit of courtship.
6. Generous use of words and ways of affection.
7. Meeting difficulties together.
8. Building a strong companionship of common interests and values.
9. A carefully worked out plan for spending.
10. Devotion to the home; owning it, if feasible.
11. Seeing the best in each other, and each other giving his best to the marriage.
12. Generous giving and taking in making adjustments.
13. Absolute loyalty and mutual trust.
14. Planning for good times together.
15. A forgiving spirit when offense comes.
16. Thinking of the happiness of the other.
17. Speaking kindly of each other's family, friends, opinions, and activities.
18. Appreciating each other's work and special interest.
19. Pray at home and give grace at meals.

20. Attending church together and sharing in the church activities.
21. A friendly attitude towards neighbors.
22. Always treating each other as very special.
23. Reverence for the sacredness of family ties.

<u>**Things That Hinder Marriage**</u>

1. Trying to boss each other.
2. Trying to make each other over.
3. Carelessness about each other's values.
4. Losing one's temper and saying bitter and sarcastic things.
5. Complaining and self-pity.
6. Criticizing each other's ideas, ways, family, and friends.
7. Ridiculing each other.
8. Putting each other on the defensive.
9. Spending carelessly and selfishly.
10. A me-first attitude.
11. Deceiving the other.
12. Taking each other for granted.
13. Unfriendly attitude towards neighbors.
14. Showing too much attention to others.
15. Carelessness in personal habits.
16. Intemperance.
17. Spending too much time away from each other – neglect.

Remembering the Marriage Vows

Each person must take the marriage vows sincerely.

> "Dearly beloved, we are gathered together here in the sight of God, and in the face of His company, to join together this man and this woman in holy matrimony, which is an honorable estate, instituted of God signifying unto us the mystical union that is between Christ and His church; which holy estate Christ adorned and beautified with His presence and first miracle that He wrought in Cana of Galilee, and is commended of Saint Paul to be honorable among all men; and therefore, is not by any to be entered into inadvisably, or lightly; but reverently, discreetly, soberly and in the fear of God. Into this holy estate these two persons presently come now to be joined. Why they may not lawfully be joined together, let him now speak, or else hereafter forever hold his peace."

The Importance of the Charge

I require and charge you with (the man and the woman) as ye will answer at the dreadful day of judgement (The marriage is recorded in heaven and will be judged in heaven, at Judgement Day.), when the secrets of all hearts shall be closed, that if either of you know any impediment (a disability that affects the validity of the marriage), why ye may not be Lawfully joined together in matrimony, ye do now confess it. For be ye well assured, that if any persons are joined together otherwise than as God's word doth allow, their marriage is not Lawful.

The man, wilt thou have this woman to be thy wedded wife, to live together after God's ordinance, in the holy estate of matrimony? Wilt thou love her, comfort her, honor her and keep her in sickness and in health; and forsaking all others? Keep thee only unto her, so long as you both shall live?

Now, let's go back and rehearse the vows: Will you love her (means to love her as Christ loved the Church). The Apostle Paul states:

> "Husbands love your wives, even as Christ
> also loved the Church and gave Himself for
> it." (Ephesians 5:25)

So, husbands we need to find out how did Christ love the Church, and then love our wives the same way. Verse 26 states:

> "That he might sanctify and cleanse it with
> the washing of water by the word."

The word sanctify (means to set apart, could it mean to use the word of God to sanctify the wife? Let's go back to the charge of the vows: love her, comfort her, honor her and keep her in sickness and in health, and forsaking all others. Keep her so long as you both shall live. Now all of that was said before you responded to the vows: <u>This is where man and woman make the vows of marriage.</u>

<u>I, the man,</u> take thee, <u>the woman</u>, to be my wedded wife, to have and to hold from this day forward, for better or worse (everything is not going to be peaches and cream), for richer, for poorer, in sickness and in health, to love and to cherish, till death do us part; according to God's holy ordinance; and thereto I plight thee my troth. "Till death do us part; sounds like marriage is forever, no matter what."

<u>I, the woman,</u> take thee, <u>the man</u>, to be my wedded husband, to have and to hold from this day forward, for better or worse (everything is not going to be peaches and cream), for richer, for poorer, in sickness and in health, to love and to cherish, till death do us part; according to God's holy ordinance; and thereto I plight thee my troth.

Then the man gives the woman a ring by putting it on her left hand and saying (which symbolizes a marriage love of eternity); with this ring, I thee wed; in the Name of Jesus Christ. Here is the final seal of the holy marriage (which is recorded by man on earth and by God in heaven). For as much as the man and woman have consented together in holy wedlock and have witnessed the same before God and this company, and thereto have given and pledged their troth, each to the other, and have declared the same by giving and receiving a ring, and by joining hands; I pronounce that they are husband and wife, in the Name of the Lord Jesus. Amen.

<u>The Ring</u>

The use of the ring, in the marriage ceremony; a man purchases for his wife the wedding ring which must be of some value. The ring symbolizes:

(1) Being circular and therefore without end, the ring is a symbol of eternity, and token of the permanence and unending happiness, which we hope and pray will characterize the marriage;

(2) The gold, unbroken metal ring symbolizes the harmony of the newly wedded couple, which hopefully will not be marred in any way.

Printed in the United States
by Baker & Taylor Publisher Services